Bipolar Dreams

An Inside Look at the Creativity
and Artistic Value of a Bipolar Mind

Stacy Lynn Stiles

PublishAmerica
Baltimore

First printing

ISBN: 1-60610-429-2
PUBLISHED BY PUBLISHAMERICA, LLLP
www.publishamerica.com
Baltimore

Printed in the United States of America

DEDICATION

My first and utmost dedication is to my muse: my husband. This book is dedicated to you in its entirety. Throughout every word, every line and every stanza, pieces of you are there. Thank you for giving me the strength, passion, and inspiration to put my feelings, thoughts and ideals on paper. I love you, Terry!

A special, heart-filled dedication goes to my beautiful daughters who have always supported my writing and who have loved me unconditionally. Thank you Autumn, Chelsea, Destinee and Mallory. Mom loves you more than life itself!

To my parents, Bill and Donna, for my existence and for loving and supporting me no matter what choices or mistakes I've made in life. I love you, Mom and Dad.

To Lisa Horton who is the amazing artist behind the front and back cover illustrations of *Bipolar Dreams*. She is a very talented writer as well. Thank you, Lisa!

Lastly, I would like to thank some of my wonderful friends at *Writing.com*. Thank you Meriki Parkinson for always being there for me through thick or thin and for always lifting my spirits and giving me hope when all hope was lost; I love you to pieces! And a very special thank-you to Sherri Gibson for your encouragement and inspiration to publish this book; you are a true, dedicated friend. I would also like to give recognition to a few other amazing friends on WDC who have always supported me and given me their friendship without asking for it: thank you Kristi Love, Kelly Petersen, Susan Stumpf, Marlena, Gabriella and Tanya. I love you guys!

BIPOLAR DREAMS

My dream is simple,
it's to become you.
Banishing this fate,
a mental state renewed.

I won't send the baggage,
that is clinging to my soul.
I'll carry on the tradition,
of being out of control.

My dream is not complex,
Alas! It's attainable indeed.
A mind free from chaos,
is all I actually need.

Even if it's for a week,
so I can see the other side.
Of a purified mental status,
not this mania which resides.

Facing the endless obstacles,
may seem a bit extreme.
But not for me, my sane one,
for all I have is dreams....

BIPOLAR FROM A TO Z

Angered by the smallest things
Bipolar disorder is my king
Conveying thoughts, hard to do
Distractions overwhelm; I'm subdued
Energy level at an all-time low
Frustration beyond reason is my foe
Going places; standing idle fast
Hanging onto "normal" visions of past
Imminent danger doesn't seem real
Justifying my reasons, unable to feel
Kidnaped my soul, without a fee
Learning to cope and trust only me
Manic depression, or so they say
Negotiating terms of a mindset betray
Oppressed memories trailing behind
Paralyzing thoughts, not hard to find
Quaintly waiting for me to confess
Raging temper at its very best
Selective my hearing, taking my soul
Tearful manipulation is my goal
Unconventional ideals; lies I must bear
Venomously I have waited, for my share
Wishfully longing for your return
X-rays show a mental psychosis learned
Yesterday's genius, today's broken plea
Zanily awaiting for my turn to be FREE!

REST AT PEACE

Another bout with danger
Staking this new wager
Creating a lust for greed
Trying to fulfill a need
Always left to hunger
Not getting any younger
Trekking down this path
Of a tiring vengeful wrath
Spending what I gain
Fighting to abstain
Actions without thought
Fearless of being caught
Chanting words of strife
No purpose left in life
Exhausted with despair
A ruthless mental lair
Anxious to break free
Disappointment sets in me
Crying to be sane
Picking at this brain
Secrets never told
Eventually will unfold
Placing blame on others
As the lies begin to smother
Taking my last breath
Finally I can rest

MANIPULATOR

Use you I will,
over and over again.
Feeding off your innocence,
endless pain about to begin.

Disposing your remains,
after I've engorged enough.
Searching for the next victim,
won't be all that tough.

Gaining what I need,
taking it at will.
You'll never stop a lion,
who's about to make its kill.

You have everything I want,
and nothing left to gain.
Let's end the petty initiation,
it's time to feel some pain.

I'll use and abuse you,
lie to get my way.
Waiting to pass on to,
the next vulnerable prey.

GOOD INTENTIONS

Time stands still, since you've suddenly gone.
I no longer see your actions of being so wrong.
I've sadly collapsed, like a broken delicate vase,
Trying to control myself, as I try to save this face.

My pulse races circles, my heart throbs for you so.
I cannot come to terms, with having to let you go.
Many years of torment, feeling so utterly damn lost.
Wanting to repair this marriage, at any given cost.

I know you had to go, feeling no emotion that day.
Now my mind's a whirlwind, what now can I say?
Such a strong woman I am, but full of emptiness.
Jealousy is my keeper, insanity I proudly profess.

How will this work, will you come back to me?
Have too many attacks, taken away your dignity?
I never meant to hurt you, yet although I did.
Feelings of solidarity, as I manage to keep them hid.

Saying responsibly, I've manipulated your trust.
I've covered my wrongs with actions, of satisfying lust.
Don't set me on this pedestal, for worthy I am not.
All the manic behavior, you simply just forgot.

I am a monster; still you don't see me as I am.
I've taken your life, using my bipolar as a scam.
Don't feel sorry for me, my intentions were true.
I thought all I wanted, was to love only you.

MY DEFENSE

I have a secret, I cannot let you know.
I'm sorry I lied; I DON'T want you to go.
Those cruel words were not how I feel,
just a defense to forget what was real.

Portraying I'm strong, with a will to thrive,
yet without you I'm lost, I don't feel alive.
Words hurt worse than punches thrown.
I'm out of control in this vicious cyclone.

So many times, you let me off the hook,
for my malicious outbursts and nasty looks.
I've used my disease as an excuse to abuse.
Flying amidst this mania, recourse I refuse.

The patience you bear, is reflective enough,
as is your wisdom, still my heart is so rough.
I want to open up and bare my entire soul,
I'm afraid all you'll see is a shallow, empty hole.

I know it was never you that gave up on us,
it was this woman you married, me in disgust.
If I could repair my mind and fix the wrongs,
I'd say you're at home, where you belong.

But we both know the truth; I'm a lost cause.
I prey on your weaknesses and all your flaws.
I'll take full responsibility for all that I am…
And remember our love, was my biggest sham….

EXCUSES OF GRANDEUR

I Sit—
In the darkness,
swaying to the ticking of the clock.
Counting the seconds passing by,
tick tock, tick tock…

I Sit—
Alone and to myself,
staring aimlessly towards the wall.
Racing thoughts now vanishing,
as my stamina starts to fall…

I Sit—
In my own sanctuary,
toiling with my whimsical ideals.
Playing a game of mental chess,
trying to mask what I feel…

I Sit—
In this recliner,
engulfed by the finest leather.
Asking myself too many questions,
feeling as light as a feather…

I Sit—
Alone in this big house,
avoiding the answers I must find.
There's nothing more convenient,
than "using" one's mental state of mind….

TELL ME I'M NOT CRAZY

Tell me I'm sane,
Tell me I'm cute,
Tell me I'm irresistible,
Tell me I'm astute!
Tell me I'm beautiful,
Tell me I'm smart,
Tell me I'm artistic,
Tell me I'm your heart!
Tell me I'm witty,
Tell me I'm secure,
Tell me I'm insatiable,
Tell me I'm pure!
Tell me I'm not crazy,
Tell me you weren't strong,
Tell me you were ignorant,
Tell me you were wrong!

TRADING PLACES

So much anger and rage,
engulf my body whole.
Can't release the tension and fury,
How was I ever to know?

No tools provided to diminish,
a path of vile and vain.
Here I bask in my own misery,
as you continue to be sane.

I detest the very sight of you,
and your precious mental state.
I detest your ambition and drive,
while I struggle against this fate.

Let's trade places today,
so you can pretend to be me.
I wonder how long you'll last,
when you're finally able to see?

See the anger, madness and rage,
through your very own eyes.
I wonder how much ambition you'll have,
as you plan your final goodbye?

A NEW ME

Today is the day,
I wash the pain away.
Plenty of soap and water,
boiling for my dishonor.

Today is the day,
I found a reason to stay.
Time is drawing near,
to face my many fears.

Today is the day,
I end my foolish ways.
Stop the mental anguish,
and your abusive language.

Today is the day,
I reason instead of delay.
Cease the blame on others,
take note of my discovers.

Today is the day,
to cut the childish play.
To allow trust in my life,
and to be your loving wife.

Today is the day,
mentally I'm not the prey.
Where I'm in control,
and finally become whole.

THANK YOU

Sometimes I feel invincible,
other times I feel minute.
Sometimes I feel powerful,
but mostly I feel mute.

Thank you for the inspiration,
from all your bitter words.
Thank you for the lack of love,
never letting my voice be heard.

Strength and will I have no more,
my mind continues to deteriorate.
Your remorse is nothing but a farce,
allegedly not trying to desecrate.

But the damage is already done,
the torment you cannot take back.
Full vicious attacks upon me,
for what you insufficiently lack.

I'M A THIEF

I'm a thief
I stole your trust
I'm a thief
I stole your lust

I'm a thief
I took your hope
I'm a thief
I took your scope

I'm a thief
I robbed you blind
I'm a thief
I robbed your mind

I'm a thief
I raided your heart
I'm a thief
I raided your smarts

I'm a thief
And I'll take more
I'm a thief
So lock your door

QUIT YOUR WHINING

Quit acting like a baby,
you're being immature.
Quit the endless drama,
your agenda's obscure.

My affection is plentiful,
you're in doubt all the time.
Let there be peace for once,
stop your childish climbs.

Enough of your tantrums,
enough of your "fits."
Obsessive needs of attention,
are old; gather your wits.

My absence is needed,
grow up and take charge.
Sacrifices you agreed to,
while I'm missing at large.

STILL SEARCHING

I'm still on the prowl
To find out who I am
A little girl still hiding
Silently fleeing on the lam

Some days I'm powerful
Other days I'm powerless
Frequently I'm exhausted
Yet yearning for success

Questioning who I am
And if "Stacy" is my name
Never feeling worthiness
Always feeling shame

Some say I'm immature
Others praise my strength
I'm still that little girl hiding
Disappearing at any length

Traces of my true identity
Flash through my mind
Trying to grasp the concept
Of releasing the child inside

These feelings of insanity
Grow stronger as I'm alone
Affection is now obsolete
Struggling to become my own

FORGET MY NAME

I felt the symptoms starting,
there was nothing I could do.
Other than up my dosage,
instead of one, ingesting two.

That didn't seem to matter,
I felt the rage beginning to mount.
An irritating aura surrounding me,
my control I must take into account.

Raged and manically inhabited,
trying feverishly to maintain control.
I lost it as fast as I wished it,
anger completely engulfing my soul.

Crying isn't going to help me,
nor are my silent pleas out of mouth.
Severe repercussions of my actions,
regret and sorrow leading me south.

As far south as my feet can take me,
escaping this cruel mental shame.
Leading me to another side of darkness,
where no one will remember my name.

PSYCHEDELIC MIND

Psychedelic shades of hue
Reds, violets and colorful blues
Shapes distorted they do convey
An imaginary delusional display

Floating matter amidst the air
Encircle my quaint modest lair
Canvas it bears no strokes of shade
Thoughts and ideals merely forbade

Rising and lifting above the roost
Lifeless serenity, no need for a boost
Psychedelic daze, peering down upon you
Your bodies so minute and I feel so new

Diminished clarity, falling quickly now
Crashing into reality, silent psychedelic vow
Teasing thoughts race ramped thru my mind
Yearning for the next trip, of an altered kind

RELEASE ME

You're a liar you will see,
the consequences that will be.
Chances taken ultimately,
damaged our souls for a fee.
Non-fundable, you have the key,
unlock the door, release me.
Aggression building openly,
loathing amidst candidly.
Thoughts of vile truthfully,
overwhelming tediously.
Take a chance, you'll soon see,
time has come to set me free.

DRESSED IN ME

Dressed in black,
a mood of dread.
Hiding my existence,
wishing I were dead.

Dressed in white,
a mood of peace.
Harmonious persona
of beauty to release.

Dressed in pink,
a mood of tenderness.
Perky and amusing,
a moment without stress.

Dressed in blue,
a mood of gloom.
Depression initiating,
for an inevitable doom.

Dressed in grey,
a mood of subtle tone.
Not quite as dark,
with a need to be alone.

Dressed in purple,
a mood of passion.
Vibrant and seductive,
yet depicting compassion.

Dressed in me,
a mood unknown.
Irritable and passive,
never carved in stone.

TOO MUCH

Too many thoughts,
and ideals to convey.
Too much emotion,
too much delay!

Trying to focus,
get my wits on track.
Too much anger,
too much slack!

Imperfections clearly noted,
mental memos in my head.
Too much deception,
too much said!

Phone ringing constantly,
not answering it today.
Too much socializing,
too much dismay!

Probing fond memories,
to offset this negative mood.
Too much solidarity,
too much being rude!

Outlines of past happiness,
appear just beyond the haze.
Too much aggravation,
too much to be conveyed!

MEDICINAL COCKTAIL

A million racing thoughts run avidly through my mind,
difficult keeping track of ideals, now unable to find!
Needing to suppress notions, all but maybe one or two,
trying to comprehend, trying to subdue!

Impossible to entirely focus on one subject at hand,
frustration, anxiety and panic attacks soon to be in demand!
Hone in on one topic; let the rest simply fade they say.
Words so easily spoken, when you're not like this every day!

Did you take your medication, or did you "forget" once again?
Let me find them for you; your moodiness is about to set in!
I don't need or want this poison, which is prescribed upon to me,
all I need is kindness and care, and finally be drug-free!

Free from this medicinal cocktail I'm forced to consume every
day, free from all the criticism; the "know it all" persona you portray!
Feed me love and guidance, not meds which leave me comatose,
I promise this time will be different, and I'll become a ghost!

I know I have stumbled and obviously let you down,
but if you give me just one wish, I'll finally be safe and sound!
I want to live life again, not needing their drugs of choice every day!
I want to be able to think clearly, without this hazy cloud of gray!

Please give me this one wish, and I'll behave myself this time!
I never thought not wanting to take drugs, would be my life of crime!
I PROMISE this time will be different and I will not need to feed,
on this poisonous medicinal cocktail, created entirely just for me!

MY INNER DEMON

There is a little demon
Which lives inside my head
When he feels like emerging
I do whatever he says

There are no scheduled patterns
No assessment, tasks or deeds
And when he shows his true colors
Nothing can fulfill his needs

His needs are very complex
Entailing endless bouts of pain
And when you think "it's over"
Still, you never feel completely sane

He'll run you through the wringer
He'll rake you through the coals
He'll take away all dignity
Leaving you defenseless, baring no soul

He hurts your loved ones most of all
Causing much suffering and pain
But once again, what else is new
Living with a person who's utterly insane

MENTAL SHOES

There is a vision inside me,
full of eternal love and mental bliss.
Is that vision so incomprehensible?
The ideal now seems so far-fetched.

What is it like to live one day,
completely insanely free?
For I cannot remember the last time,
my disease didn't entirely consume me.

Control and patience they say,
these remedies seem very far and few.
Just walk a path of insanity once,
inside my mental shoes.

I DON'T CARE

Who cares about your feelings
Who cares about the truth
Who cares about your social status
I don't care that you have proof

Leave me alone and dwell in your sorrow
I have enough to deal with on my own
Think of yourself and no one else
Your disposition has once again shown

Talk about all your accomplishments
Talk about your many troubles in-depth
Let's not forget all of your precious deeds
Or how many times because of me you wept

I no longer care if you don't understand
Or your questions on why I can't just be sane
I don't care if you ever come to the realization
That my disease to you is not just a simple bane

I don't care if you think you hold the power
And my entire life remains in your hands
Your support has been a complete mimicry
Now it's my turn to set the final demands

A TIME FOR HEALING

My memories are bleak
   they're dormant in my mind
   resisting thoughts of childhood
pretending to be blind.

Insecure by your actions
   which left me isolated and alone
   all because you could not refrain
taking what you didn't own.

Panged with insatiable hunger
   to be free of your restraints
   hiding behind a mask of fear
on a canvas of abuse I paint.

Palettes filled with colors
   of the darkest known to man
   brush strokes with a purpose
to cover what began.

I've seen you since that day
   you took my innocence by hand
   eyes looking off into the distance
as in front of you I stand.

Emotionless you stood there
   unable to look me in the eyes
   glancing into a haze of darkness
of your deepest lies.

Look at me, this woman now
    who stands before you unafraid
    the one you trespassed against
as a child you betrayed.

Don't look off into the horizon
    acting as though it didn't exist
    a wretched, foul example of a man
a soul that won't be missed.

LOVE FOUND A WAY

A childhood basked in the essence of sheer betrayal.
Through the eyes of innocence, love found a way.

Damaged, not completely broken by the memories.
I am the woman I am today, for what you did to me.

Abuse, pain and torture, from my lover yet I stay.
Through the eyes of madness, love found a way.

Amidst those eyes of hatred, a daughter it did bring.
Beautiful and dainty, a painful heart now proudly sings.

Vicious shots of venom, at my cost and my dismay.
Through the eyes of verbal abuse, love found a way.

Each poisonous word out of mouth, helped me realize
The loving husband persona was only a crafty disguise.

A psychological diagnosis, as if I were on display.
Through the eyes of insanity, love found a way.

Creativity blossoming with the passing of each word.
Articulate with a passion for my life's saga to be heard.

A past full of trauma has made me who I am today.
Through the eyes of victory, love found a way.

Life has many trials which all of us must endure.
But love will find a way to open those closed doors.

ONLY WORDS

To you they're only words,
uttered out of anger.
To me they're forceful stabs,
with a jagged dagger.

Stating I've lost my will,
along with any drive.
Shouting I have no purpose,
nor will I ever thrive.

Begging me to forgive,
for only human you are.
Promising you'll try to end,
this brutal vocabulary war.

But like any other battle,
one must try to succeed.
Realize I'm not the enemy,
it's me you cause to bleed.

"They're only words" seems
to be your favorite line.
Even when I've begged you,
to see the abusive signs.

You'll never change, will you?
This is who you are.
My only words left to say,
I can no longer bear the scars.

CHILDHOOD TEARS

You took and you took,
until I could give no more.
You corrupted my childhood,
abducting the youth I adored.

I tried to remain focused,
forgiving each and every day.
But your abominations towards me,
left me empty and betrayed.

It's easy to say I forgive you,
even though a part of me never will.
It's easy to say I've forgotten,
the trauma which you instilled.

But I keep pushing forward,
though the trials seem so tough.
You've stripped away my dignity,
making me callously rough.

Years you've taken from me,
impossible to ever give them back.
Silently suffering by myself,
for your ruthless brutal attacks.

I've gathered all my courage,
I shaved off all my fear.
Now all I see is the beauty,
of the Lord brushing away my tears.

BIPOLAR REALM OF REALITY

Irritable and frustrated.
Very easily distracted.
Trying to come down,
from a high overacted.

Understand it's not my
desire, to react as such.
Care instead of claiming,
bipolar is just a crutch.

The mania has subsided,
my better half setting in.
Depression now knocking,
with its dark smug grin.

Darkness now my master,
he's once again on time.
Binding me to this torment,
of a mental state of crime.

Help is no longer an option,
I asked you manias ago.
Stating it's all in my head,
this craziness that I show.

I did educate with reason,
asking you to listen openly.
You dismissed me as usual,
and my menial constant pleas.

If there's one thing I've learned,
over the course of my disease.
You have to love yourself,
you're the only one you have to please.

BROKEN

Yes I'm broken
   but not beyond repair
   tragically I've endured
your lies and mental despair.

Did you really think
   you'd completely break
   me, when you've seen
that I'm clearly not that weak.

I'm no longer that
   vulnerable woman you
   married many eons ago
thinking you could still subdue.

I'm wise to your contempt
   and the constant looks of
   self-righteous bitterness
when the push has come to shove.

Taking what you want at will
   vehemently you demand
   that everything goes your
way with a wicked show of hand.

This routine has become old
   as so have you, my dear
   and yet you still don't
get it, love was your greatest fear.

So yes, I am broken
   I've begun to fix what's been
   done, the damage you've created
I will find myself once again

I LOST MY WAY

True intentions
   Fill my soul

So much ambition
   So many goals

Searching for answers
   Longing to find

My purpose in life
   Future in mind

Marriage and children
   At a young age

Beautiful daughters
   Take center stage

Schoolwork and activities
   Now my success

Friends and sleepovers
   Bedroom's a mess

Youthfulness leaving
   Becoming mature

Lessons I've taught them
   Morals secure

A mother I've been
   I lost my way

Towards my goals
   I was led astray

But am I disappointed
   Of choices I made

The path I chose in life
   I'd never trade

THE ROAD TO NOWHERE

It seems I've traveled this path,
too many times to count.
A road which leads to nowhere,
mentally unable to dismount.

It was an easy route to follow,
for demands were not in place.
The only requirement needed,
was precious time to waste.

As I follow the road of surrender,
thoughts tease my mental state.
Is this the path I'm destined for,
and have I sealed this fate?

I should have turned around,
and taken an alternate route.
But rationalizing the purpose,
left me full of doubt.

The path less traveled is easier,
than walking towards one's goals.
The road which leads to nowhere,
will embrace this empty soul.

FAR FROM HOME

It seems like an eternity,
since you left our home.
Residing in this new country,
wandering aimlessly to roam.

Carefully plotting your mission,
jotting mental notes every day.
Repressing traumatic memories,
cautiously watching what you say.

You've succumbed to isolation,
watching the enemy close.
Performing guard duty nightly,
patrolling your nightmares the most.

Planning has become a ritual,
your schemes are now in play.
Searching the stars for answers,
praying for just one more day.

One thing you failed to realize,
as you patrol this endless roam.
Your body is now here with me,
but your mind is still far from home.

UNDER ATTACK

How long have you waited,
for the memories to cease?
How long have you suffered,
as they took piece by piece?

I've seen the emotion and anguish,
in your heart and in your eyes.
I've heard the horrid events,
on the news and thru your lies.

You tell me it wasn't that bad,
as the media described it to be.
You tell me that living in Iraq,
was a small price paid to be free.

But I don't see you liberated,
I see a man who's lost and alone.
Still under attack each night,
silently residing in a combat zone.

Our lives have forever changed,
your heart has turned to black.
Suffering by yourself in solitude,
as you wait for the next attack.

OUR QUEEN

She is the queen, the queen of lies!
She sits on her throne, masked in disguise.
Manipulation and dishonor she solemnly seeks,
from her loyal servants and those who are weak!

She basks in the scent of deceitfulness,
as you foolishly believe, you will progress!
Bearing the fruits of her followers' labor,
portraying her façade as though it's a favor!

Her mission is simple to all who can see,
her lust in life, is to promote only "me"!
You sit in suffrage, as she commences to excel,
stating there's a mission too important to tell.

The queen has spoken, we all must abide,
a wonderful queen who has never lied!
She sits on her throne surrounded by many,
graceful and wise, with a look so canny!

But her guidance has failed, along with her lies,
she has set the precedent of a dying enterprise!
A queen so beautiful, who used her charm,
to prey on the weak and cause much harm!

Exiled from a throne, for your lies of deceit!
Lack in leadership skills has caused your defeat!
Had you been caring, and not thought of only you,
we would still honor the grace of our queen of taboo!

TREASURE HUNT

Love is a treasure, all of us may hold,
it carries us through life, never to be sold.
It shows us mercy while other attributes do not,
solaces our soul and simply can't be bought.

Treasures we are seeking, monetarily so to speak,
a priceless gift of eternity, is love when at full peak.
All the riches in the world cannot fill the empty void,
the only key to happiness is love when truly enjoyed.

It will never leave you, though pain is a side effect,
one dose of erroneous love, your heart will fully reject.
It gives you guidance and helps in times of need,
a bond never to be broken, an emotion flows to feed.

Yes, it can be agonizing and at times let you down,
as quickly as it dissipates, a new love again is found.
Protects your vulnerabilities and eases your mind at rest,
love is never taking, giving is what it does best.

Treasures we may be seeking subconsciously in our minds,
clearly taking for granted a wonderful gift so easy to find.
Use your gift wisely, don't misuse it or discard to the side,
your treasure has been with you, in your heart, deep inside!

BIPOLAR IN DOUBT

I've enjoyed many successes,
even though my mind plays tricks.
Thoughts vanish as fast as they come,
and here I stand transfixed.

A racing mind is very difficult,
to keep focused and alert.
Anxiety is my shadow,
no happiness, just disconcert.

Can one control the thoughts,
that never seem to stop?
The ones that overwhelm you,
the thoughts too hard to drop.

Wishing for an end to this,
all the suffering and pain.
Knowing nothing's here for me,
and nothing left to gain.

Do I hold the answer?
Have I misled myself?
Maybe I'm not that different,
perhaps I'm like yourself.

AUTUMN HAS ARRIVED

Crisp chill of the brisk morning air,
trees formerly full are now virtually bare.
Vibrant colors of many and striking hues replace,
the lavish lively greens, previously once in place.

Autumn has arrived with her presence aglow,
an artistic colorful palette of beauty to show.
Leaves falling gracefully onto the frosty ground,
falling ever so hastily, creating a glorious mound.

Children running delightedly awakened with cheer,
for colorful mounds of leaves are ever so near.
Jumping in one by one, the leaves do tell a tale,
of a once fearless oak, who now looks so frail.

Basking in the essence of autumn's sweet delight,
her loveliness remains a glorious imminent sight.
Enjoy her virtuous nature as her absence draws near,
another season vanished, as winter suddenly appears.

ARTISTICALLY DISEASED

Yes I am bipolar,
though to me it's not a curse.
My life could have been different,
it could have been much worse.

I don't perceive my disease,
as a curse; rather, it's a gift.
For it illuminates my senses,
and that artistic desired lift.

Many are forced to succumb,
believing they cannot succeed.
My outlook is just the opposite,
all expectations I will exceed.

So when you think it's over,
and your mind has taken a toll.
Remember that "gift" inside of you,
is one you completely control!

THE WALK OF LIFE

Young, vigorous and full of life,
these are my adolescent years.
Neither worry nor a care,
no visions of the upcoming fears.

Charismatic, virtuous and free,
stunning as a fully blossomed rose.
These are my teenage years,
no responsibility; just a stunning pose.

A young mother, a young wife,
built around chaos and constant despair.
These are my early twenties,
no fear of aging, yet the times drawing near.

Career-oriented and focused,
my beauty still remains.
The captivation which once drew a crowd,
is slowly fading in vain.

My early thirties have come upon me,
with insecurities running amok.
Sadly all I felt I had was beauty,
and certainly I've been struck.

Beauty, fame and fortune,
something all of us wish to gain.
But not at the cost of our loved ones,
and not at the cost of someone else's pain.

I have taken a new outlook on life,
as the years unavoidably pass me by.
My first priority is family and friends,
and learning to laugh until we cry.

So in the end, what matters the most,
is it fame, fortune and personal gain?
Or is it the moments we share with our friends,
and the family which still remains?

SURVIVAL OF THE SANEST

The race began the moment,
we took our very first breath.
The race in life called sanity,
from newborn to inevitable death.

Obstacles and debris surely,
discouraging the lengthy path.
Keep yourself entirely focused,
steer clear of the toxic wrath.

Embrace life's little wonders,
don't misuse the simplest show.
For struggle is here to greet you,
as you stroll through plentiful woes.

Don't become disappointed,
or throw up your hands in disbelief.
Troubles and emotions will certainly,
cause you abundances of grief.

Take the negativity and use it,
as an advantage instead of plight.
Never give in to the weaknesses,
your victory is clear in sight!

SUCH IS LIFE

Some are blessed from birth, scarcely needing to try,
others work an entire lifetime barely getting by.
New blisters forming daily, bodies taking a toll,
nothing left to sacrifice, but a tired empty soul.

No planning ahead, for the future seems so bleak,
parody of the working man trying to make ends meet.
Lack of education, but hard-working with hands of steel.
Sunrise to sunset he works to provide his family a meal.

Underprivileged, inflated with debt, his spirit soaring high.
Gazing over his loved ones, his body releases a heavy sigh.
What will tomorrow bring, is a promised raise soon to arrive?
A lucky break is all he needs to ensure their ability to survive.

Struggling has become a ritual, they're very accustomed to.
Apologizing to his wife, "I'm sorry this was the best I could do."
Her eyes filled with tears, taking him by the hand without strife.
"My love was never monetary, for YOU are my reason in life."

HAPPIER PLACE

I know most of my poetry seems dark and somewhat bleak,
But if you notice my darkest writes are always when I'm weak.
My poems about my children are always that of a positive set,
It's the ones about my childhood, which portray a past regret.

Feelings and emotions can vanish as quickly as they appear,
So one must prepare themselves with pen and paper always near.
Reminiscing about the past is somewhat good for the soul,
Even memories involving pain, writing helps us grow.

I'm really a cheerful person and negativity you'll rarely find,
It solely depends on the mood I'm in, and my current state of mind.
Certain topics and actions, can trigger an episode of my disease,
Negative intentional comments and stressors meant to tease.

So when I speak about my loved ones, love surrounds me whole,
Your criticism merely provides me with an important essential role.
Lashing out on paper, emotions I cannot express to your face,
Are only thoughts at the moment, which take me to a happier place.

GAME OVER

The game is over, you win; I willingly throw in my hand
The cards have been stacked in your favor, exactly as planned
I know the stakes were high and maybe I folded too fast
But I no longer want to play this game I know will never last

I've already lost too much and more I cannot spare
So no longer deal the cards my way, the game was never fair
I'll count my blessings early, leave this table of deceit
For a game already prejudged is a game I cannot defeat

A sore loser I'm not, just tired of the same outcome
Petty to most of the players, important to a lecherous bum
Would have stayed in had the cards been shuffled right
Instead the cheating was displayed within my sight

So game over, I renege and throw in my hand
I'm starting my own new game, not previously planned
Fair, consistent and honest; my game will entail all of this
Entertaining each new player, this table of love will never dismiss

THE JIGSAW PUZZLE OF LIFE

One big happy family is an understatement at best,
A mother whose devotion has built this frenzied nest!
A morbid sense of humor, dedicated to our throne,
Without this main piece of puzzle, our fate would be unknown!

Our father is a comedian, in every sense of the word,
His selflessness and compassion, feeling invisible, never heard!
Cussing, ranting anxiously at the simplest tasks in life,
Never thinking of himself, just his children, grandchildren and wife!

The oldest sibling out of three is a hard-working soul,
An entrepreneur in every sense, always achieving any goal!
Passive and lenient his family comes first, always giving his time,
Working seven days a week well within his prime!

The middle child, only daughter, stuck between two boys,
Never feeling appreciated, trying to fill a void!
First to go to college, becoming educated and well-known,
Still searching for a sense of belonging, though she's now all grown!

The baby of the family and that baby still remains,
With his lack of responsibility and spending what he gains!
With the heart of a lion, he's very strong and very brave,
Just a tad bit naïve in life, just waiting to be saved!

Four grandsons and eight granddaughters keep the puzzle intact,
Nonstop adventures and activities, always running within a pack!
One has gone off to college, the remainder will follow her lead,
Instilling values upon our children, always teaching them to succeed!

Our children are our future and our family may be a little insane,
But for one to finish this puzzle, one must first experience some pain!
Our puzzle is completed and the pieces create a perfect fit,
This jigsaw puzzle of memories, is a piece of history to submit!

JUST WRITE

Just write, they say,
an essay or an article.
Poetry is just a hobby,
nothing short of a miracle.

Just write your essays,
continue as you've done.
Stating you like my poetry,
but it's merely just for fun.

Just write your journal entries,
continue to nourish your mind.
Your poetry is cute, my dear,
but it's simply silly rhymes.

Just write, they say,
and that's just what I'll do.
They're blinded to the purpose,
of writing poetry for reviews!

ANOTHER MIRACLE

Life surrounds us with miracles each and every day,
blinded are the many not seeing the wonder displayed.

A child born with ten fingers and ten perfect toes,
a child free from illness and healthy as he grows.

A single mother struggling to ensure they survive,
endless obstacles; her child's health promotes her drive.

A troubled lost soul in dire need of a helping, loving hand,
suicidal thoughts disappear, and now forever disband.

An atheist whose religion is filled with hatred and disbelief,
taking his last breath, the Lord's love fills his voided grief.

An elderly couple's family is misplaced and out of touch,
a deserted puppy, who's love has given them so much.

An abused neglected child dwelling inside a house of dead,
blessed is the hero, who saves this child of dread.

A once-successful entrepreneur who lost everything he had,
homeless in need of shelter, a "nobody" lends him a hand.

Miracles are all around us, if we only take the time to see,
the next one in need of a miracle could surely be you or me.

YES, THERE REALLY
ARE MONSTERS

Growing up as a child, I never wanted to sleep alone.
Fearful of the isolated darkness and mostly the unknown.
"Mommy, are there monsters?" a question I would commonly ask.
"Only on Halloween, my dear, the ones we see in masks."

Still not satisfied with her answer, I questioned her more.
Asking her the same old thing as I did the night before.
Frustrated and exhausted, she took me by my little hand.
Looking under my bed, in my closet, even the night-stand.

"So see, my daughter, the monsters are only in your head.
It's time to get some sleep Stacy Lynn, now do as I have said."
Respecting Mommy's wishes, my little body trembling with fear.
Wishing the hour was morning, praying for "him" not to appear.

But as darkness faded, an uncomfortable silence fell about.
I could hear the monster stirring, preparing to come out.
Hoping the noises I heard were my brothers fooling around.
Pulling covers tightly over my head, praying not to be found.

Footsteps getting closer, the monster is at the foot of my bed.
I hear his heavy breathing, this is not at all what Mommy said.
Quietly lifting covers back, he lays down in the bed beside me.
Touching, groping and mauling, covering my eyes so I can't see.

He took away my childhood and my trust and self-esteem.
A pleading child without a voice, invisible as it would seem.
"So yes, my daughter, there are monsters, everywhere we look."
Stating as I remembered my childhood and everything he took.

GUILTY

Corrupted and tainted,
tarnished from my past.
A heart full of wrongs,
made me this outcast.

Shameful my actions,
desired with fault.
Mistaken objectives,
cast a brutal assault.

Withered and worn,
this heart on my sleeve.
Lusting for power,
thirsting to deceive.

Besmirched is my mind,
smugly you grin.
You believed your abuse,
had completed your win.

The remorse I feel,
is all because of you.
Tantalizing the weak,
ensuring I withdrew.

Now here I am older,
no longer the gullible child.
A heart vacant of bitterness,
a mind now beautifully beguiled.

I WIN...

YOU'RE GONE

Screaming to be free
Detesting all of me
Wishing you were here
Drowning in my fears
Crying to be whole
Loathing your new goals
Fighting to survive
Longing to feel alive
Struggling with this fate
Trying not to hate
Smothering all this pain
Explosive once again
Combating this new plot
Hoping I'll get caught
Probing feelings naught
Tasting hateful lots
Pleading for your help
Banish hurtful yelps
Dejecting the unknown
I'm tired of being alone

YOU CAN'T TAKE BACK

You can't take back the tears I've shed,
you can't take back the words you said!

You can't take back the loneliness in my heart,
you can't take back the feelings to depart!

You can't take back the endless lies of deceit,
you can't take back the miles of defeat!

You can't take back the torture I've endured,
you can't take back the insecurities you've ensured!

You can't take back the disloyalty to me,
you can't take back the demeaning debris!

You can't take back the selfish displays,
you can't take back the relationship of decay!

You can't take back the need to dominate,
you can't take back the destruction you did create!

You can't take back the chaos and mental despair,
you can't give me back wasted minutes, days, and years!

SYMBOLIC LIES

Representation you do depict,
of a crafty liar who does subsist.
Can't keep focused in any type of thought,
feared of being noticed, feared of being caught.

A figure so grand, yet honesty you lack,
stature appealing, strangers you attract.
Charisma and charm attached as well,
if they get close, dishonesty they'll smell.

Reeking of deceit, an aroma engulfs you whole.
The price you'll pay will be your entire soul.
So try to fool them, portray yourself as not,
your lies will catch up to you, never to be forgot.

Your contentious state has no remorse to show,
astounding as your dignity has vanished ever so slow.
So try to fool them, for I know who and what you are.
Time is nearing quickly for an unwittingly charm disbar.

LOSING SIGHT

You bring out the worst in me,
I knew it from the start.
Careless slips of the tongue,
as if you had no heart.

I'm walking down a path,
I've already hiked previously.
Swearing time and time again,
I'd never lose sight of me.

Yet here I am, once again,
with fears and emotions amok.
Reverting back to same old me,
mentally drained and out of luck.

Does a pastime of mental abuse,
condone my progressive ignorance?
How can I say I'm completely healed,
when all I still feel is this?

So, the healing process died,
along with my dreams today.
I lost again, the marathon of hope,
now all I can do is pray.

LOVE ME, LOVE ME NOT

I don't care what you say,
I confess there'll come a day!
When you are taken down a notch,
pray forgiveness, watch your watch!

You can take me or leave me,
either damn way!
You don't have to like me,
nor do you have to stay!

Love me you will for all I've done,
sacrifices made, you've made none!
You think I'm bossy, I think you're rude!
You think I'm moody, I think your crude!

Dislike who I am and ignore the signs,
dismiss my pleas and worthless lines!
Respect you will, this you owe to me,
I've endured the hardships and the misery!

You, the King of disregard and of ignorance!
Me the Queen of contemptuous, remarks of bitterness!
You don't have to like me, but love me you will,
our vows of matrimony, are dwelling with us still!

NEVER ENOUGH

I've lived my life, not for me,
I've lived my life for my family.
Putting their needs always first,
I truly love this faithless curse!

I'm a giver and never do I take,
here's our love, a total disgrace.
My heart is pure and full of love,
all I ask for is help from above.

The Lord had a special plan,
the very minute my life began.
Why hasn't it been employed,
or has it already destroyed?

I pray that He will heal,
my wounds and all my ideals.
I'm losing faith as time goes by,
I'm losing hope that "this" won't die.

I pray to Jesus, "Please hear my pleas,"
I pray He'll show them what He sees.
Everything I do, is never enough,
all I do for YOU, is never that tough!

Open his eyes and let him see,
that the woman in dire is vainly me!
Show him the sacrifices I have made.
Show him just how much I have prayed!

Everything I do is never my best,
anything I do is a constant protest!
Please help me, Lord, to remain strong,
please help him, Lord, show him he was wrong!

YOU SAY

You say you're right,
I say you're wrong.
You say I'm weak,
I say I'm strong!

You say I'm difficult,
I say I'm fair.
You say I'm irritable,
I say you're unaware!

You say I'm manic,
I say you're blind.
You say I'm angry,
I say I'm fine!

You say I'm psycho,
I say I don't care.
You say I'm needy,
I say my share!

You say I'm immature,
I say you're the child.
You say I'm a bitch,
I say I'm mild!

You say I'm losing it,
I say it's already gone.
You said you'd help me,
I say you were wrong!

KARMA

Lucky for me,
fortunate for you.
We found our destiny,
intentions so true!

Chances we took,
accidents on cue.
Caressing so cautious,
words misconstrued!

Our fate bound,
our luck running out.
Careless we whisper,
outcome in doubt!

Is this coincidence,
meeting by chance?
I never felt the karma,
of love at first glance!

DEFINING ME

I don't want to be,
one of those girls.
Relying on a man,
constant fiscal swirl.

I am independent,
most of the time.
But all can be weak,
relying on a dime.

I don't need a man,
to define who I am.
I just need confidence,
I don't give a damn!

I don't wish to be,
one of the many.
Where gifts are given,
and count the pennies.

So here I sit alone,
the girl with plenty.
Non-monetary items,
with the love of many.

CRIED OUT

I can't cry,
the tears won't fall!
Dried up forever,
a built-up wall!

You can't hurt me,
I'm too numb to feel!
The lash of your sting,
this time is surreal!

I've lost the ambition,
and drive to do right!
I've lost the admiration,
and the willpower to fight!

I can't cry,
my tears have disappeared.
I can't give you back,
what you stole over the years!

YOU WON'T SEE ME

I'm masked within a stranger's skin,
and walk amidst the massive crowd.
My lips as soft as silken strands,
my existence is not allowed.

I don't stand out above the rest,
though appearances can deceive.
What you see is not who I am,
seeing only what you believe.

A child, mother and sister lives,
within these dark and shallow walls.
A friend, lover and confidante,
always there to cushion the falls.

Yes, I'll falter and, yes, I'll fail,
invisible to all I see.
Yes, I'll fumble and, yes, I'll plead,
for someone to see the real me.

You won't see me, I'm a delusion,
deep in the back of your mind.
You won't see I'm exactly like you,
for lack of insight has rendered you blind.

INFECTED

Contaminated—
By everyone I've
ever touched.

Diseased—
By every heart
I've ever clutched.

Tainted—
This vessel has
begun to decay.

Soiled—
Excessive damage
I portray.

Insane—
Manic and
ready to bust.

Crazy—
No one left
for me to trust.

Dirty—
My mind and
soul combined.

Infected—
Diseased and
left behind.

EXHAUSTED AVENUES

Spent energy,
no drive.
Droopy eyelids,
must revive.

Need sleep,
too much to do.
Running errands,
losing you.

Cradling memories,
yesterday's past.
Sensing distance,
falling fast.

Love for life,
children first.
Endless devotion,
now we're cursed.

I won't change,
this is me!
Lost in a tug of war,
too blind to see....

I HATE YOU

Is it a sin to say I hate you,
even if this is how I feel?
Lack of remorse and empathy,
your reaction simply unreal.

I was raised never to say this,
with values and morals in place.
Yet, I cannot help feeling like this,
my life with you is such a waste.

I hate you more than anything,
these feelings I cannot hide.
You see it when I look at you,
foolishly tossing it to the side.

I was raised to be better than this,
and never say hurtful things.
A sin to me would be hiding,
the hate inside and what it brings.

So yes, I definitely hate you,
and every little thing you portray!
I hope you have a good back-up plan,
the romance is over and swept away!

HALL OF SHAME

Walls filled with memories, of yesteryears galore,
a painted rugged picture, I'd never seen before.
Regretful ignorant actions, portrayed on display,
of a remorseful shallow entity, induced to betray.

Trinkets, awards and certificates, also nil to show,
of all of my achievements, as you watched me grow.
Photographs are missing, no proof on hand to confirm,
a struggling adolescent, with no conscious left to affirm.

Was I ever special to you, or was I simply another face?
My wall of space is empty; was I that much a disgrace?
I walked the hall of memories, in search of one positive set,
but all I found was sadness, with a shameful recurring regret.

I bow my head looking down, at the straps upon my heels,
never glancing upwards, humiliated by what the hall revealed.
A non-existent being, with a past so invisibly out of sight.
A disgraceful, putrid portrait, of bitterness and infinite contrite.

I walk along the hall of shame, dreadfully longing for the end.
Taste of dishonor overwhelming me, as you still condescend.
I saw a beautiful ray of light and a loving hand did then appear,
guiding me through my empty past; humiliations slowly disappear.

He softly takes me by the hand and begins to take the lead,
fingertips still search the wall, for a past accommodating deed.
For one swift moment I saw a glimpse of previous glorious days,
the hall of shame disappearing, as I finally remember my name.

MY DESTINY

If I would have had a crystal ball and seen what lay ahead,
making wiser choices, than taking the easiest path instead.

What I chose was a destiny, filled with turmoil, abuse and pain,
yet had I been the wiser one, the hidden sanity would still remain.

I keep telling myself to look ahead and leave the past behind,
trying to escape haunting memories is a task I'm unable to find.

Still feeding off the memories of a relationship gone bad,
staying trapped inside these emotional walls is all I've ever had.

Moving forward, still upset, that life has let me down,
basking in old memories, submersed and left to drown.

Waking from this nightmare with eyes open and aware,
my past was just a segment, of a mental psychosis we both shared.

CHARM ATTACK

A fool I am this is entirely true
For being the one who fell for you
Falling so hard without a safety net
Hitting rock bottom, still waging this bet

Charming and dashing, charismatic too
Not seeing the person who was really you
Masked behind a smile and those pretty eyes
A perfect display of horrors able to disguise

Proclaiming to be a man who never did exist
Plotting your scheme, you're unable to resist
Bad boy persona women are instantly drawn to
Me, the chosen one out of many surrounding you

But now I know the truth and honor I do not feel
I'm returning this gift immediately so I can heal
I do not wish to exchange or get my "money" back
Keep it for the next prey who'll welcome this charm attack

THE LOYALTY BOND

How kind of you to think of me
On this beautiful autumn day
Were your thoughts regarding your loyalty?
Or were they thoughts rehearsed to display?

Such a powerful thing, this loyalty bond
Something we all inevitably yearn
A bond of trust and fidelity
A bond which we all must earn

Many will take it lightly
Most will not understand
Some will honor and embrace it
Yet the majority will heartily disband

I laugh at the thought of the loyalty bond
The yearning of a bond which does not exist
It's amazing how all of us will long for
An illusion so easily dismissed

I FAILED

I thought I could help you,
what a whimsical scheme.
Already set in your ways,
what far-fetched dream.

You're still the man,
you proclaim to hate.
Why do I even try,
this winless debate?

I shouldn't have wanted,
to change who you were.
Even as you asked for help,
I knew there was no cure.

So fail you I did,
for an impossible task.
Make peace with yourself,
you never should have asked.

I'M STILL ME

Who I was,
Is who I am.
What I said,
was not a scam.

I'm still me,
I've not replaced—
My true identity,
It's still in place.

Look deep inside,
You shall see.
Your daughter, your sister,
All of me.

Don't be confused,
By subtle change.
I've only adapted,
To this life of derange!

I REMEMBER

Remember when our love,
was thoughtful and so kind?
The endless times you made me laugh,
now I see that love is blind.

Remember all the power you held,
with one embrace and passionate kiss?
All the endless laughter,
and the sweet essence of reminisce?

Remember our passion and care,
over the simplest things in life?
The very moment you asked me,
to be your faithful wife?

Remember how much you loved me,
showing me with actions instead of words?
Our overzealous displays of affection,
the idea now simply seems absurd.

Remember how considerate we were,
a very long time ago?
The supportive tone of our voices,
gentle, without a despicable show.

Remember when you said "I do,"
for now and eternity?
How we vowed to love each other,
to which both of us agreed?

Remember the endless tears we shared,
over the many losses in our lives?
Always stating nothing would change,
now we're struggling for "this" to survive?

I remember...

DEPARTED FRIENDS

Where does one draw the line,
on a friendship gone astray?
Does one pretend it's coincidence,
or perceive it as an act of sheer betray?

Where were you when I needed you,
and yearned for your comforting voice?
For as I recall, my best friend,
my loyalty to you was never a choice.

Throughout all the pain and suffering,
the laughter and the tears,
My love remained unconditional,
over the course of many years.

Can you state the same for me, my friend,
my sister always within my eyes?
For one can't base friendship on coincidence,
Which has now led to our fatal demise.

Our memorable days are far gone now.
Our paths have parted us in separate ways.
One on a mission of self-destruction,
the other on a mission to pray.

Pray for me as well, my friend,
my sister, best friend and confidante.
For those deemed not worthy of prayer,
are the ones who are mostly forgot.

BROKEN PROMISES

Opened the door foolishly; welcomed you home again
Promising me that this time a newborn man you've been
Your criticizing, cynical nature has vanished, left without a trace
Sensitivity, kindness and compassion, characteristics now in place

Anger and temperament have dissipated, this I swear to you
No longer the tyrant of conflict and now know what I must do
Words so easily spoken from a man who can't bear an nth of remorse
A newfound saga slowly diminishing on his self-destructive course

Promises are meant to be broken and you are the champion of this
Actions speak louder than words and as always a typical remiss
Obnoxious, boisterous and controlling, change you have not made
Assurances from a master manipulator, broken oaths of promises betrayed

Aggressive approaching stature, disregarding the ones proclaiming to love
Loyalty and commitment vanishing as I pray to the Heavens above
Lord, please stop this abuse and cruelty, keep me safe and sanely sound
For this troubled man will not leave me, his honor is not loyally profound

Please provide the guidance I need to rebuild this broken soul
My faithfulness is diminishing and I'm pleading to once again be whole
Your child I am perpetually and the air I breathe is because of You
Please, my Lord, remove this man, his departure is well overdue

GRANTED IT WAS MY CHOICE

Granted I held the "know-how"
To make decisions on my own
I knew the consequences
Of being afraid to be alone

Granted I was raised with values
And morals to guide through life
I had the opportunity
Of remaining the invisible wife

Granted I knew right from wrong
Yet somehow I veered off path
I knew the fundamentals
Of an addictive ruthless wrath

Granted I abused your advice
Tossing it to the side as simple dismay
I knew the truthfulness
To which my actions did display

Granted I took your kindness
And took advantage without remorse
I took your loving admiration
Allowing my tenacity to run its course

Granted I was weak and I failed again
To the many immoral decisions I see
It was my choice to undo the past
But in the end it was all because of me

REPENT

Egotistical, you're on a high
Uttered words, always a lie
Self-centered, you're such a joke
Arrogant as always, love to provoke

Narcissistic aura all around you
Vainly existing, best you can do
Haughty appearance, expected display
Selfish behavior deceives every day

Egocentric nature, beyond approach
Insensitive actions, nil reproach
Thoughtless impressions gaily displayed
Conceited instructions always replayed

Superior your stature devouring you whole
Smug manifestation, feeding your goals
Self-righteous portrayal, very evident
Overconfidence consumption; never to repent

HYPOCRITICAL GALORE

Who are you to demand my trust?
I'm the one who lacks the lust!
You're the one suffering in life,
I'm at peace, your faithful wife!

Who are you to believe your lies?
Telling us to be loyal and wise!
Actions speak louder, words are dismissed!
How asinine of you to always insist!

Insist we behave in a manner you approve,
Proclaiming we all need to highly improve!
What about the demons knocking at your door?
Shall we turn our heads to a hypocritical galore!?

Always are you right, never are you wrong,
An unfathomable an idea, yet feel so strong!
A narcissist perhaps, for you love only you.
We sit as hostages waiting upon your queue!

We no longer wish to play your delusional game,
Escaping this crisis will be our "minute of fame!"
Narcissist and hypocrite, describe you the best
Pray for His forgiveness when you finally come to rest!

LOST IDENTITY

Give me your trust
You owe it to me
I haven't faltered lately
And I hold the key

A few small mistakes
Why do you care?
Respect my authority
Cast away your despair

You're so immature
When will you grow up?
So I haven't been truthful
You need to suck it up

Mind games I play
Day in and day out
Forget your intuitions
You're ridiculously in doubt

The task is very simple
Do as I say and not as I do
I control all the power
To cast my spell over you

Now that I have you
Completely under my spell
Forget the family you had
Bid them all farewell

I have many plans for you
You'll finally see the light
Forsaking all our enemies
Your will is gone to fight

I'll take care of you
As I always have you'll see
Don't worry about my methods
For the process is to become me

I'M SORRY, GRANDPA

I'm sorry, Grandpa, for exposing the putrid ugly past
I was only seeking closure now that you have passed
But looking back I forgot to mention a few important facts
Like the love and care you shared and how you always kept a pact

Keeping a secret was one of your attributes remembering to this day
Like the time you kept that secret from Mom without a moment's delay
Your untimely visits to our work, forcing all of us to take a break
Bringing us treats and cold beverages, encouraging all of us to partake

Sweet memories I can remember of a grandfather who believed
That his granddaughter held the potential to pursue any of her dreams
I know your life wasn't perfect or even semi-somewhat sane
I know you also lived a lifetime of your own torment, abuse and pain

The past is not what defines us as to who we are today
It's merely a small segment left to us how we choose to convey
Forgiveness I have learned even though it took me years
Holding back suppressed memories, holding back the tears

Strength I have gained as the years have come and gone
Ending this futile battle, standing ever so proudly not withdrawn
So I'm sorry, Grandpa, for expressing just one memory of the past
Your granddaughter loves you dearly, the pain is finally over at last

ALONE

So many friends and family,
yet I'm so isolated and alone.
No one to reach out and talk to,
all by myself left to condone.

How did I let this happen again,
why didn't I see it a mile away?
How did I allow the trap to be set,
knowing my past foolish ways?

I guess what he said is the truth,
and I am completely truly insane.
Look at the foolish choices I made,
I just can't help not to refrain.

I'm attracted to the conflict,
and sickly to all the pain.
When will the violence stop,
and end this life of disdain?

Measly all I've ever ask for,
is just one single beautiful day.
A day where my complicated life,
is not in complete disarray.

I sugarcoat my troubles,
and most of all my despair.
Dwelling in my own misery,
not willing or able to share.

So here I sit in solitude,
trying to work my troubles out.
Conversing with my thought process,
always a second doubt.

It's hard to get good advice,
from an unstable mind.
Not knowing if I'm right or wrong;
fearful of what I'll find.

Can I maintain this relationship,
when only one will communicate?
It's hard not to take the easy way out,
though it's becoming one of my traits.

I don't feel I'm evil, though,
maybe I've been wrong all along.
I do want to be normal,
but I first need to become strong.

So here I sit in solitude,
with this pen and paper in hand.
They've now become my new best friend,
and they always understand.

I NEED AN ANSWER

Where did it go?
Why couldn't it last?
How could it all crumble,
so incredibly fast?

Bitter yet satisfied,
with a turmoil of haste.
Such a vacant relationship,
what a terrible waste.

I'm crying on the inside,
alone and left to dwell.
A life full of misery,
an empty outer shell.

You infested my mind,
manipulated my thoughts.
Love we once shared,
never could be bought.

I don't know the answers,
to my questions of spite.
The only recourse I have,
is to continue this fight.

AUTUMN

I cannot explain in words, the love of a daughter so dear
For she's taken away my heart, and left me in utter fear

The fear of her growing up, and leaving this abode to grow
To grow into someone else, without my guidance to bestow

My life I would give for her a hundred-thousand times
Endless love to give and endless love to assign

She has a precious gift, a gift in which nothing can compare
She brightens up the world, and takes away all misery and despair

Her eyes are a mystery as to who she will become
My little baby girl has completely come undone

Her freckles are now beauty marks,
her rosy cheeks are now filled with rouge
What happened to that little girl who is now destined to never lose?

So please, my child, don't leave me, but if you do have to go…
Remember this mother's love for her daughter will forever
continue to grow

ONCE UPON A PAIR
OF BIG BROWN EYES

I gave you all beautiful brown eyes, all in which I could give
I taught you the meaning of love,
patience and kindness, and always to forgive
Your beauty, your charisma, your humor,
that all came deep from within me
So why is it, my beautiful brown eyes,
a special bond between us will never be?

Don't ever let them fool you or indefinitely lead you astray
For this precious gift I've given you, no one can strip away
Remember who you are and what the meaning of life truly is
And remember, beautiful brown eyes,
how our lives have now come to this

You won't realize it today, tomorrow or perhaps for years come
But what I've given you is life, my daughter,
and that can never be undone
You are and always will be my beautiful brown-eyed bundle of joy
But your faithfulness and commitment now simply seems a ploy

I no longer have the energy or the will to try and make you understand
That your life has evolved so quickly and I'm no longer a part of your plan
I tried with all my might to be the best mother that I could be
And even though I made mistakes,
your identity cannot be taken from me

For you are and always will be my daughter, no matter what they say
And although you've let me down and hurt me,
that's my life each and every day
So what shall happen next, my beautiful brown-eyed gift in life?
Will you remember what I gave to you or will you simply take it
into strife?

I've given you so much, so much in which you cannot openly see
For your blinders have now rendered you thoughtless of what
you're doing to me
I have finally come to the realization that the time has come to let you go
But it seems as though the time went by so quickly,
yet I know it's time for you grow

So don't worry about my feelings or emotions,
which are now completely arrayed
For you will always be in my thoughts,
my prayers and my heart each and every day
You've become a woman now, my beautiful gifted brown-eyed child
And nothing can erase the precious moments we shared and all
times we smiled

TABOO

Never speak the truth
Keep it bottled up inside
Never speak the horror
It's something I must hide

I can't release the pain
That was caused upon to me
I can't release the mental anguish
And the endless years of misery

What is a societal taboo?
When all I speak is the truth
Why do so many people shun
What is so clearly putridly uncouth?

Write about all cheerful things
Never about your past
Write about sunsets and rainbows
Forget and allow the hurt to pass

I'm sorry, but I can't do that
I was sexually molested as a child
Three adult males
Took my innocence as they smiled

Forgiveness I have given
To each and every one
But the pain and scars I still bear
Over the mental abuse that they have done

WAS IT LOVE?

Respect you lack,
for you and I.
Careless your actions,
a symphony of lies.

Look me in the eyes,
as you stutter words.
I see the deception,
of a persona absurd.

Think back long ago,
our love was there.
Spreading like wild fire,
I remember, I swear.

Though, maybe it was I,
enamored by you….
Maybe I was in love,
and you never had a clue.

HELP ME, PLEASE

Help me, please,
I'm falling apart.
Make me invisible,
give me a new start.

Help me, please,
I'm out of control.
Make me an illusion,
life has taken its toll.

Help me, please,
I'm at my wits' end.
Make me disappear,
it's too far gone to mend.

Help me, please,
I'm lost and alone.
Make me imperceptible,
guide me through the unknown.

Help me, please,
this deadness won't leave.
Make me evaporate,
help me believe.

Help me, please,
get my mind on track.
Make me the woman I was,
before I made this pact.

Help me, please,
his presence is my demise.
Make me realize,
I failed after endless tries.

Help me, please,
my future's now bleak.
Make me appreciate,
the love that I seek.

IF I COULD ERASE IT ALL

If I could take back,
everything I said.
I'd do it in a heartbeat,
retracting every single thread!

If I could erase the words,
and place them where they belong.
My eraser would then dissipate,
as I feverishly erase the wrong!

If I could turn back the clock,
and reluctantly go back into time.
I would think about the consequences,
of writing a hurtful rhyme!

But reversing time isn't an option,
So, I'm searching for another mode.
To be able to say to you, "I'm sorry"
I give you this single pleading ode!

STRANGER IN MY BED

Who is this strange man laying beside me?
You're not my lover and I'm not the enemy.
Searching and probing for a familiar touch,
Wanting and needing it just a little too much.

Where is the man I married prior to this war?
I want him back entirely as he was once before.
They tell me he's changed and it will never be,
But loving him so much, I tend to disagree.

Heroically fighting, for our freedom abound,
Risking his life, for a cause to be unfound.
Solitude and silence is one of his demands,
Still mentally residing, in that far distant land.

Shelled and mortared each and every night,
Unable to sleep for the fear of needing to fight.
Scorching and exhausted, feeling empty and alone,
Representing invincibility, wanting to come home.

Exploring and probing to find the man you used to be,
Trying to discover similarities, trying to remember me.
I've been with you entirely, even when you were gone,
I never left your side even though you've now withdrawn.

What will it take for this stranger to up and leave?
How long must you isolate? How long must we grieve?
Our children need you desperately as so do I,
Don't let the memories destroy you, allow them to subside.

Come home again and thrust this stranger out.
He's been dwelling too long, his reign is over, no doubt.
You've served this country honorably without remorse,
It's time to come home and allow our marriage to run its course.

I will not give up and abandon you, nor will I give in.
Fight for our family's loyalty as you did so back then.
I'm tired of sleeping alone, with this stranger in my bed.
I want that loving, caring man; I want my husband back instead.

I WONDER

Do you think a person's past,
defines who they are today?
Or merely small chapters in life,
with choices to portray?
Can irrational behavior be excused,
by a mental diagnosis?
Or should one be accountable,
for a psychological neurosis?

Do people really forgive,
even if the person's a child abuser?
Or is it one step closer to insanity,
of the manipulative user?
Do we deem ourselves as martyrs,
when we enforce the law?
Can we say beyond a doubt,
our judicial system is without flaw?

Is true love only true,
during first stages of the romance?
And after twenty-five years,
will it still be love at first glance?
Can people really change,
or is that something the foolish hope?
Are they sadly grasping at straws,
while at the end of their rope?

Would you still love me,
if my outer appearance was not as so?
Could you hide disgust in your eyes,
and would you let me go?
Is your love unconditional,
when I've seen you walk away?
How come when I needed you most,
you fled and did not stay?

Did you give enough and realize,
the importance of your life?
Did you praise the Lord and thank Him,
for making me your wife?
If you leave this world tomorrow,
can you say you have no regrets?
Or will your soul be troubled,
casting a cold shadowed silhouette?

NIGHTMARES

When I close my eyes to sleep,
I pray to dream happy thoughts.
Every night reads alike for me,
Endless battles I have fought.

Disturbing as one could imagine.
Partial derangement is all I share.
If I allocate more than a glimpse,
It would now be your nightmares.

Dreaming of death and torment,
Evil rituals to say a few.
I feel painful stings of every gash,
Closing my eyes to what they do.

Hideously they show their faces,
In plain view, not out of sight.
Tempting my powers of elation,
Mentally slaying me every night.

Some dwell within the shadows,
More deadly than the evident.
Wickedly laughing towards me,
Reeking of sinful, raunchy scents.

When I close my eyes to sleep,
I pray for a spirit of peace over me.
To fight and win this battle of flesh,
And one day be nightmare-free.

IMPRESSED WE'RE NOT

Who and what you are,
is nothing to be proud.
Lacking the sensibility,
obnoxious shouts aloud.

I know what you sadly seek,
and the evil that clearly exists.
Surrounding your body entirely,
with a wicked show of fist.

Your stature is all you have,
proud of being so large.
Intimidating those around you,
excessive need to be in charge.

No one is impressed,
by the toughness and brawn.
So find another method,
to cover all your wrongs.

SEASONS OF LIFE

New seasons come, and then pass away.
Each brings their beauty for another day.
Yearning to feel the warmth of their depth,
Longing to value what we cannot accept.

Life is like the seasons, with a tale to tell,
Each bearing their passions, incredibly well.
The budding of spring, brings much hope,
With a knack to thrive, and a drive to cope.

Summer warms the soul, and all her seeds.
Nourishing life, with a very special need.
Bathing in her beauty, basking in the sun,
Living life to the fullest, another day is done.

Fall has begun the transformation process,
As trees become barren with leaves of less.
Impressive colors and hues on display,
Gorge in the splendor as long as they stay.

For frigid winds and blistering cold is near,
To banish the warmth and bring in the year.
Winter is so bold, and proudly represents,
A season of chill, with the darkest torment.

Seasons of life smile upon us, deeply with care,
Sharing their vital gifts, promoting our prayers.
As one season dissipates, another one derives,
With a stunning sensation for enriching our lives.

ENTER AT RISK

Walk up the drive,
pebbles and stones.
Rose bushes align,
all beautiful tones.

White picket fence,
pillars in place.
Flourishing gardens,
such charming grace.

Off in the distance,
afar is one single tree.
Black and deadened,
now all I can see.

Wind blowing shutters,
hard against the house.
Dimming darkness,
obscurity doused.

Sign posted near,
on a rusted oval disc.
Letters so boldly,
"Enter at Risk"!

ABUSIVE FATE

Unfaithful useless utter
Demeaning devoured décor
Violent vicious venom
Mockingly medaling more

Creative cautious coalition
Against all amidst abate
Struggling sanely satisfied
For a ferocious frigid fate

Dominate destructive deity
Proud pacifying past
Loathing lustrous lividly
Fictitiously falling fast

Gallantly ghastly grounded
Remaining reluctantly recluse
Distance desired deadliness
Amusing agonistic abuse

OUR CREATION

Loco lonely liaison
Passionless painful prize
Who we were withering
Erroneous empty eyes

All alone aimlessly
Sitting silent suffering
Soulless stranger sadly
Ruthless regretful ring

Astute audacious affection
Brings betrayed blasphemy
Pleading posing practicality
Misleading mental me

Destruction deviated distance
Afar against all advice
Cries crafting compassion
Disarmed disloyal device

ALL HALLOW'S EVE

Ghouls, ghosts and goblins
wicked witches wielding.
Spirits soaring sacredly,
trick or treating?

Pumpkin patches present,
barren by butcher's beast.
Careless costumed children,
foul frightening feast.

Darkened distressed demons,
patiently persecuting prey.
Evil engulfs the entities,
devouring delicious day.

Halloween howls heard,
from foreign fetched fans.
Yearning, yielding, yenning
heinous helping hands.

EVERYDAY FORECAST

Broken buried bond,
regretful recurring rain.
Pouring putridly passionless,
provocative priceless pain.

Falling furiously fast,
ominous oath to obey.
Torrential teary torment,
conventional course conveyed.

Submersed soul stammering,
darkness deadening distantly.
Drowning deep disarray,
methodically mocking me.

Laughter lingers lucidly,
Submerged suffering sight.
Treading thoughts tenaciously,
for a fruitless fearful fight....

SCENTS OF DREAMS

Dreams dying distantly,
long lingering light.
Falling further faraway,
fabricated fouled fight.

Traces teasing telling,
selfish senseless sores.
Open oafish obedience,
crackling coastal core.

Sacrificial senses stating,
an awkward abandonment.
Naked notions needing,
succulent selfless scents.

Aromas airing anonymously,
teaching the tale to tell.
Dislocated dreams deadening,
a fictional final farewell.

SOLITUDE

Staring at the same four walls, each looks the same
Orating silently to myself a destructive faceless bane
Loneliness is settling in with each ticking of the clock
Isolation is what I seek, a submissive mental block
Teary eyed with sadness for wanting nothing more
Uselessness surrounds me, lying lifeless on the floor
Destined to be secluded, control lies within my hands
Empty sheltered venue, waiting only upon my command

MOLESTED

Manipulated into thinking I know not right from wrong
Overpowered by his stature, my weakness makes him strong
Loathing the thought, the time has come to go to bed
Escaping all the nightmares, forcing them to the back of my head
Sexually deviant and wicked, he's completely out of control
Twisted are his thoughts, as he finally takes my soul
Evil vicious cycle, spinning round and round and round
Devastation lasting a lifetime, still waiting to become unbound

DYSFUNCTIONAL FAMILY

Disarrangement overwhelms our company
Years of family tales to tell
Scars from previous battles
Fierce conviction handed down so well
United in chaotic conditions
No responsibility for actions revealed
Careless actions healed
Typical disorganized reunions
Irrational behavior tightly sealed
Order is not on the menu
Nor the tranquility we all long for
A slice of bitter pie we offer
Longing to indulge the sour pastry more

Forever we're united
As all family members should be
Maybe my family's not perfect
Innocent love is all I see
Leaning on each other's shoulders
Yet we're always going to disagree!

INVISIBLE

Ignorant to the favoritism, a desire to be special too
Naïve to the sarcasm and criticism, finding it easy to subdue
Validity still not broken, as I feverishly try to understand
Insanely searching for something, waiting upon your command
Silence numbs my body, reaching out for a delusion to hold
Imperfect vanishing appearance, a love so wrongfully cold
Brazen on the outside, while dying on the inside all alone
Love is all I ever yearned for, not this affection carved in stone
Eagerly waiting for a sign, yet fearful of what I may find….

SHUT UP

Stagnantly idle, all can see
Horrifying comments, said to me
Utterance of ignorance, because I disagree
Thunderous demands, broken debris

Unkempt existence, useless plea
Piercing is the voice, an obnoxious potpourri

STYLES

Saddle back shoes or shag if you please
Trends by the thousands, hair as big as you can tease
Yoga and yo-yos; Yuppies the majority of the crowd
Leggings and Levi's; colors vibrant and loud
Eyelashes as fake as the breast upon your chest
Styles they come and go as we try to look our best

HIGH MAINTENANCE

High heeled leather pumps, the best will only do,
In various styles and colors, the most brilliant of hues!
Gorgeous diamond jewelry, a temptation not to resist,
Hone my very essence and surely enhance my wrists!

Managing hair appointments, a color and highlight is a must,
Angelic to the naked eye, beauty is what we lust!
Imperfections not visible, expensive makeup applied to disguise,
Neiman Marcus and Marshall Field, fully stocked with vital supplies!
Tanning bed awaits, a special bronzer first I must get,
Enriched with vitamins and minerals, top-shelf purchase let's not
forget!
Nylons hosiery and lingerie, Victoria's Secret now exposed,
A variety of silk and satins, frilled with lacy garnished bows!
New car smell in the air, a fast sporty convertible is what I seek,
Candy-apple red adorning the most expensive leather seats!
Exhausting idea of being a perfect wife, beauty is a weakness on this
path of life!

SEXUALLY MOLESTED

Self-esteem destroyed, lost and never found
Engaged in unwanted advances, provocatively I am bound
X-rated is the action, painfully unable to forget
United are the demons, which created the mood to set
Audacity running through his veins, unable to see the fright
Losing all my dignity, fighting with all my might
Lusting for a purpose, one of the ultimate sins
Yearning for gratification, not thinking of the child within

Mortified beyond repair, a terrified child now resides
Ominous words of silence, a perfect secret now to hide
Losing this perverted battle, feeling mute and all alone
Emptiness has now replaced, a subtle joyful tone
Silence I have learned, haunting memories hiding within
Trust I give to no one, for all of life is one big sin
Exiled from a childhood, which made me who I am today
Disgraceful haunting memories…as my childhood fades away

BIPOLAR

Belligerent and irritated by almost any little thing.
Insaneness surrounds me; craziness is what I bring.
Psychosis is not the problem; the problem lies within.
Overzealous personality; much absorption sinking in.
Liar, cheat and manipulator; trust you should not give.
Ambition at its lowest; no longer wanting to live.
Racing thoughts; try to unwind, ultimate goal for unstable minds!

CPSIA information can be obtained at www.ICGtesting.com
Printed in the USA
BVOW03s1111290714

360869BV00001B/44/P